CELEBRATING THE CITY OF MIAMI

Celebrating the City of Miami

Walter the Educator

Silent King Books

SILENT KING BOOKS

SKB

Copyright © 2024 by Walter the Educator

All rights reserved. No part of this book may be reproduced in any manner whatsoever without written permission except in the case of brief quotations embodied in critical articles and reviews.

First Printing, 2024

Disclaimer
This book is a literary work; the story is not about specific persons, locations, situations, and/or circumstances unless mentioned in a historical context. Any resemblance to real persons, locations, situations, and/or circumstances is coincidental. This book is for entertainment and informational purposes only. The author and publisher offer this information without warranties expressed or implied. No matter the grounds, neither the author nor the publisher will be accountable for any losses, injuries, or other damages caused by the reader's use of this book. The use of this book acknowledges an understanding and acceptance of this disclaimer.

Celebrating the City of Miami is a little collectible souvenir book that belongs to the Celebrating Cities Book Series by Walter the Educator. Collect them all and more books at WaltertheEducator.com

USE THE EXTRA SPACE TO TAKE NOTES AND DOCUMENT YOUR MEMORIES

MIAMI

In Miami's embrace, where the sun does gleam,

Celebrating the City of
Miami

A city of magic, where dreams convene,

Palms sway in rhythm, to the ocean's theme,

In this tropical paradise, life is serene.

A skyline like a painting, in the twilight's glow,

Neon lights ignite, where the breezes blow,

From Biscayne Bay's depths to Art Deco's show,

Celebrating the City of
Miami

Each moment in Miami, a new story to bestow.

The Everglades whisper, ancient and grand,

An ecosystem thriving in this fertile land,

Mangroves guard secrets, waters so unplanned,

In this wilderness' cradle, nature takes a stand.

Streets vibrate with cultures, from all far and near,

Cuban beats in Little Havana, you'll hear,

Diverse voices unite, with joyous cheer,

Celebrating the City of
Miami

In this melting pot city, love conquers fear.

South Beach's allure, where sands are white,

Under moon's gaze, the nights are bright,

Dancers in motion, till dawn's first light,

In Miami's heartbeat, passions ignite.

Ocean Drive hums, with classic cars' glide,

Fashion and glamour, where the worlds collide,

Artists and visionaries, here they reside,

In this haven of creativity, dreams don't hide.

Wynwood Walls, where murals breathe,

A canvas of life, where artists bequeath,

Stories in colors, from joy to grief,

In Miami's pulse, every wall is a sheath.

The flavors of the city, a feast so grand,

Arepas, ceviche, a taste of each land,

In markets and kitchens, with expert hand,

Miami's cuisine, a cultural strand.

Seabirds circle o'erhead, in skies so blue,

Pelicans dive, and the dolphins too,

Coral reefs below, a world so true,

In Miami's embrace, the old and new.

Beneath the night's velvet canopy,

City lights twinkle, a radiant spree,

In Miami's dreamscape, harmony,

Of past, present, future, eternally.

Celebrating the City of
Miami

ABOUT THE CREATOR

Walter the Educator is one of the pseudonyms for Walter Anderson. Formally educated in Chemistry, Business, and Education, he is an educator, an author, a diverse entrepreneur, and he is the son of a disabled war veteran. "Walter the Educator" shares his time between educating and creating. He holds interests and owns several creative projects that entertain, enlighten, enhance, and educate, hoping to inspire and motivate you.

Follow, find new works, and stay up to date with Walter the Educator™
at WaltertheEducator.com

www.ingramcontent.com/pod-product-compliance
Lightning Source LLC
LaVergne TN
LVHW012050070526
838201LV00082B/3901